How to Dazzle at

SCIENTIFIC ENQUIRY

Richard Barnett and Derek Green

Brilliant Publications

We hope you and your class enjoy using this book. Other books in the series include:

Science Title:

How to Dazzle at Being a Scientist   978 1 897675 52 6

English Titles:

How to Dazzle at Writing   978 1 897675 45 8
How to Dazzle at Reading   978 1 897675 44 1
How to Dazzle at Spelling   978 1 897675 47 2
How to Dazzle at Grammar   978 1 897675 46 5
How to Dazzle at Romeo and Juliet   978 1 897675 92 2
How to Dazzle at Macbeth   978 1 897675 93 9
How to Dazzle at Twelfth Night   978 1 903853 34 4

IT Title:

How to Dazzle at Information Technology   978 1 897675 67 0

Maths Titles:

How to Dazzle at Algebra   978 1 903853 12 2
How to Dazzle at Maths Crosswords Book 1   978 1 903853 38 2
How to Dazzle at Maths Crosswords Book 2   978 1 903853 39 9
How to Dazzle at Oral and Mental Starters   978 1 903853 10 8
How to Dazzle at Written Calculations   978 1 903853 11 5

Published by Brilliant Publications,
www.brilliantpublications.co.uk

Sales and despatch:
BEBC (Brilliant Publications), Albion Close, Parkstone, Poole, Dorset BH12 3LL, UK
Tel: 01202 712910   Fax: 0845 1309300   Email: brilliant@bebc.co.uk

Editorial:
Brilliant Publications, Unit 10, Sparrow Hall Farm, Edlesborough, Dunstable,
Bedfordshire, LU6 2ES, UK

The name Brilliant Publications and its logo are registered trademarks.

Written by Richard Barnett and Derek Green
Illustrated by Pat Murray
© Richard Barnett and Derek Green 2003
ISBN 978 1 903853 15 3
First published 2003, reprinted 2004, 2007.
10 9 8 7 6 5 4 3

Contents

Unit no.	Title	Scientific Enquiry 1			Scientific Enquiry 2																page
		a	b	c	a	b	c	d	e	f	g	h	i	j	k	l	m	n	o	p	
7A	Pollen tubes				X																8
7B	Christopher's height												X		X						9
7C	Woodland birds													X							10
7D	Animals in leaf litter									X											11
7E	Stomach ache								X												12
7F	Burning candles																	X			13
7G	Gas, liquid or solid															X					14
7H	Pure salt								X	X											15
7I	Electric light bulbs						X														16
7J	Burning foods										X										17
7K	Rubber bands												X	X							18
7L	The seasons													X							19
8A	Trying to slim				X																20
8B	Circulation	X				X															21
8C	Yeast												X								22
8D	Yellow fever			X																	23
8E	Dandelions							X	X												24
8F	Element or compound?		X																		25
8G	Freezing points								X												26
8H	River deposits				X									X							27
8I	Comparing limestone									X											28
8J	Pans																		X	X	29
8K	Electromagnets															X					31
8L	Measuring reflections												X								32
8M	Investigating hearing																		X		33
9A	Woodlice													X	X						34
9B	Catch it																		X	X	35
9C	Counting bubbles												X								36
9D	Duckweed								X												37
9E	Neutralization												X								38
9F	Bubbles from metals																X				39
9G	Acidic or alkaline soil											X									40
9H	Burning magnesium												X	X							41
9I	Ideas about burning	X																			42
9J	Current						X														44
9K	Gravity								X												45
9L	Parachutes				X																46
9M	Turning forces												X								47

Introduction

How to Dazzle at Scientific Enquiry contains 41 photocopiable sheets for use with 11–14 year olds working mainly at levels 3–5. The activities as a whole help students to acquire the experimental and investigative skills required to conduct successful science investigations. They can be used whenever the need arises for particular activities to support and supplement your existing scheme of work for science. The activities provide learning experiences, which can be tailored to meet individual student's needs.

The activities are addressed directly to the student. They are self-contained and many students will be able to work with little additional support from you. You may have some students, however, who have the necessary scientific skills and concepts but who require your help in reading the sheets.

All the activities are set out on photocopiable sheets with spaces for the completion of answers, the production of tables and the plotting of graphs, etc.

How to Dazzle at Science Enquiry relates directly to the programmes of study for Experimental and Investigative Science. The contexts for the activities are derived from the programmes of study for Life Processes and Living Things, Materials and their Properties and Physical Processes. Each activity links directly to a particular unit in the QCA scheme of work for Key Stage 3 Science. The activities have been written to supplement this scheme. The QCA scheme of work is designed so that certain units in each year cover attainment targets 2–4. These are as follows:

Units A–D – Life Processes and Living Things
Units E–H – Materials and their Properties
Units I–L – Physical Processes

The contents grid on page 3 gives details of the activities for each unit. The shading in the grid shows which aspects of the Scientific Enquiry programme of study are addressed in each activity. In addition, the investigative focus of each activity is indicated with an 'X'.

Links to the National Curriculum

How to Dazzle at Scientific Enquiry supports the following elements of the programme of study.

Sc1 Scientific Enquiry
Ideas and evidence in science

1 Pupils should be taught:

    a about the interplay between empirical questions, evidence and scientific explanations using historical and contemporary examples (for example, Lavoisier's work on burning, the possible causes of global warming);

    b that it is important to test explanations by using them to make predictions and by seeing if evidence matches the predictions;

    c about the ways in which scientists work today and how they worked in the past, including the roles of experimentation, evidence and creative thought in the development of scientific ideas.

Investigative skills

2 Pupils should be taught to:

Planning

    a use scientific knowledge and understanding to turn ideas into a form that can be investigated, and to decide on an appropriate approach;

    b decide whether to use evidence from first-hand experience or secondary sources;

    c carry out preliminary work and to make predictions, where appropriate;

    d consider key factors that need to be taken into account when collecting evidence, and how evidence may be collected in contexts (for example, fieldwork, surveys) in which the variables cannot readily be controlled;

    e decide the extent and range of data to be collected and the techniques, equipment and materials to use (for example, appropriate sample size for biological work);

Obtaining and presenting evidence

    f use a range of equipment and materials appropriately and take action to control risks to themselves and to others;

    g make observations and measurements, including the use of ICT for data logging (for example, variables changing over time) to an appropriate degree of precision;

    h make sufficient relevant observations and measurements to reduce error and obtain reliable evidence;

    i use a wide range of methods, including diagrams, tables, charts, graphs and ICT, to represent and communicate qualitative and quantitative data;

Considering evidence

j use diagrams, tables, charts and graphs, including lines of best fit, to identify and describe patterns or relationships in data;

k use observations, measurements and other data to draw conclusions;

l decide to what extent these conclusions support a prediction or enable further predictions to be made;

m use their scientific knowledge and understanding to explain and interpret observations, measurements or other data, and conclusions;

Evaluating

n consider anomalies in observations or measurements and try to explain them;

o consider whether the evidence is sufficient to support any conclusions or interpretations made;

p suggest improvements to the methods used, where appropriate.

The activity sheets are designed to support students working mainly at levels 3–5. The level descriptions below taken from the Science National Curriculum indicate what skills are required at each level. Only levels 3–5 for attainment target Sc1 have been included.

Attainment target 1: Scientific Enquiry

Level 3

Pupils respond to suggestions and put forward their own ideas about how to find the answer to a question. They recognize why it is important to collect data to answer questions. They use simple texts to find information. They make relevant observations and measure quantities, such as length or mass, using a range of simple equipment. Where appropriate, they carry out a fair test with some help, recognizing and explaining why it is fair. They record their observations in a variety of ways. They provide explanations for observations and for simple patterns in recorded measurements. They communicate in a scientific way what they have found out and suggest improvements in their work.

Level 4

Pupils recognize that scientific ideas are based on evidence. In their own investigative work, they decide on an appropriate approach (for example, using a fair test) to answer a question. Where appropriate, they describe, or show in the way they perform their task, how to vary one factor while keeping others the same. Where appropriate, they make predictions. They select information from sources provided for them. They select suitable equipment and make a series of observations and measurements that are adequate for the task. They record their observations, comparisons and measurements using tables and bar charts. They begin to plot points to form simple graphs, and use these graphs to point out and interpret patterns in their data. They begin to relate their conclusions to these patterns and to scientific knowledge and understanding, and to communicate them with appropriate scientific language. They suggest improvements in their work, giving reasons.

Level 5

Pupils describe how experimental evidence and creative thinking combined to provide a scientific explanation (for example, Lavoisier's work on burning). When they try to answer a scientific question they identify an appropriate approach. They select from a range of sources of information. When the investigation involves a fair test, they identify key factors to be considered. Where appropriate, they make predictions based on their scientific knowledge and understanding. They select apparatus for a range of tasks and plan to use it effectively. They make a series of observations, comparisons or measurements with precision appropriate to the task. They begin to repeat observations and measurements and to offer simple explanations for any differences they encounter. They record observations and measurements systematically and, where appropriate, present data as line graphs. They draw conclusions that are consistent with the evidence and begin to relate these to scientific knowledge and understanding. They make practical suggestions about how their working methods could be improved. They use appropriate scientific language and conventions to communicate quantitative and qualitative data.

Pollen tubes

Most plants reproduce by pollination. During pollination a bee or other insect transfers the pollen grain (the male sex cell) to the ovule (female sex cell). When the pollen grain lands on the female part of the plant it grows a tube. This tube takes the male sex cell to the female sex cell.

You can grow pollen tubes by placing pollen grains in sugar solutions. Pollen tubes will grow better in some sugar solutions than others. Plan an experiment to find out what strength of sugar solution is best.

1. Make up a question that you can then investigate.
   Use the following key words or phrases to help you.
   what   *strength*   *sugar solution*   *best*   *pollen tubes*   *grow*

   _____

   _____

2. To make your investigation fair,

   a. what will you change (vary)?

   _____

   _____

   b. what will you keep the same?

   _____

   _____

3. How will you change (vary) the strength of the sugar solution?

   _____

4. How many different strengths of sugar solution will you use?

   _____

5. How many pollen grains will you put into each sugar solution?

   _____

6. How long will you leave the pollen grains in the sugar?

   _____

7. What equipment will you use to see the pollen tubes? What results will you write down?

   _____

Add-on
Design a table to write down your results.

Christopher's height

Christopher is now aged 17. The table below shows how his height has changed since he was 5 years old. What can the table tell you about how Christopher has grown?

Age (years)	Height (cm)
5	106
6	114
7	119
8	125
9	130
10	136
11	141
12	145
13	149
14	154
15	170
16	181
17	186

Plot a bar chart of the results to present the data.

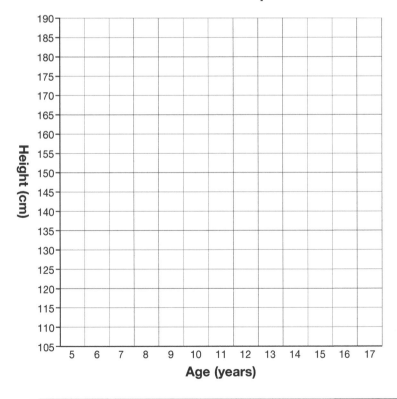

1. At what age was Christopher growing fastest?

_____

2. If Christopher had been measured when he was 9½ years old, what height do you think he would have been?

_____

3. What height do you think Christopher will be when he is 18 years old?

_____

Add-on

What do you think the word 'puberty' means?

Woodland birds

A year 7 class wanted to see if there was a relationship between the level of light and the level of sound in the woods in their school grounds. They recorded changes in the light levels using a light sensor during one day in the spring. They also recorded the sound level in the woods on the same day using a sound sensor. Birds singing made most of the sound.

The class drew this graph to show their results.

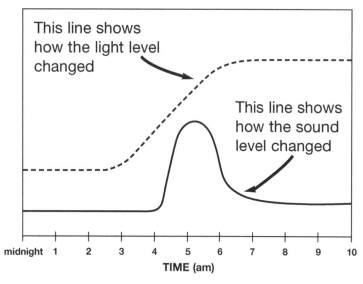

This line shows how the light level changed

This line shows how the sound level changed

midnight 1 2 3 4 5 6 7 8 9 10

TIME (am)

Use the graph to answer these questions.

1. The birds started singing at 4am. At what time was the birdsong loudest?

_____

2. Between what times shown on the graph was the light level the highest?

_____ and _____

3. The pupils thought that increasing daylight in the morning could be a signal for the birds to start singing. Can you explain how the information in the graph supports this idea?

_____

_____

4. What do you think happens to the level of birdsong during the evening?

_____

Add-on

The class only collected data about sound and light levels for one day. What do you think they could do if they wanted to be more certain about their results?

Animals in leaf litter

Pupils in a year 7 class had been looking at the different types of small creatures that could be found living in the leaf litter under a hedge. Each group was then asked to compare two creatures and write down two similarities and two differences between them. This would help them identify the creatures better.

Joanne and Kamal compared an ant to a centipede.

 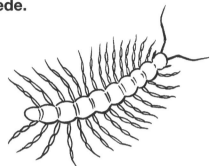

Here are the similarities and differences Joanne and Kamal came up with.

Similarities

○ Both animals have legs.

○ Both animals have a pair of antennae.

Differences

○ The ant has only got 6 legs but the centipede has got 30.

○ The ant has got 3 body segments but the centipede has got lots of

Mike and Dhanishla decided to compare an earwig to a weevil.

 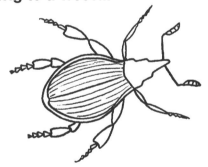

Write down two similarities and two differences that you can see between these two animals.

Similarities	Differences
1. _____	_____
2. _____	_____

Stomach ache

Laura and Louise were arguing about indigestion tablets. Both girls thought their own tablets were the strongest and best. They decided to plan an investigation to find out who was correct.

Answer the following questions to help you plan an investigation.

1. What causes indigestion?

_____

_____

2. What would you add to each tablet to test them?

_____

_____

3. How can you make your comparison of the tablets fair since each tablet might be a different size?

_____

_____

4. What other things must you keep the same to make your investigation fair?

_____

_____

5. How would you know when the tablet has 'worked'?

_____

_____

6. What safety precautions will you need to take during your investigation?

_____

_____

Add-on
Draw a diagram of the equipment you will use.

Burning candles

If you place a glass container over a burning candle, soon the candle will go out. It's easy to time how long it takes for the candle to go out. George made a prediction.

The bigger the glass container, the longer it will take for the candle to go out.

Volume of glass container (ml)	Time for the candle to go out (s)
100	0.5
250	1.2
400	1.8
500	1.9
750	3.4
1000	4.6

He repeated the test with six glass containers of different sizes. These were his results:

Plot a line graph of George's results.

1. On the graph add a line of best fit. This is a line that goes through most of the points to show the pattern of George's results.

2. Were any of the results anomalous? (An anomalous result is one that does not fit the pattern of the rest of the results.)

   On the graph, draw a ring around the result you think is odd.

3. Can you think of a reason why George might have got an odd result?

Add-on

How could George improve his investigation to reduce the effect of odd results?

Gas, liquid or solid

Substances can be a gas, a liquid or a solid. Carbon dioxide is a gas. Read the information given about carbon dioxide and then produce your own information about water and brick.

Gas
Example: **Carbon dioxide**

○ Carbon dioxide is an invisible gas.

○ Carbon dioxide is the gas used in fizzy drinks.

Properties that tell you carbon dioxide is a gas:

1. You can squash it.

2. It will spread out to fill its container.

How the particles are arranged

Bubbles of carbon dioxide in a fizzy drink

The particles of carbon dioxide are spread out with lots of space between them

Liquid
Example: **Water**

○ _____

○ _____

Properties that tell you water is a liquid:

1. _____

2. _____

How do you think the particles would be arranged?

Solid
Example: **Brick**

○ _____

○ _____

Properties that tell you brick is a solid:

1. _____

2. _____

How do you think the particles would be arranged?

Pure salt

Rock salt is a mixture of sand and salt. Yvonne and Sahil worked out a way to get pure salt from rock salt. They did this in three stages. Read through their notes and look at the diagram they drew for the first stage. Then draw labelled diagrams for stages 2 and 3.

Stage 1: Dissolving the salt

○ We put the rock salt in a beaker.

○ We added 100cm^3 of warm water to the beaker.

○ We stirred the mixture until all the salt had dissolved.

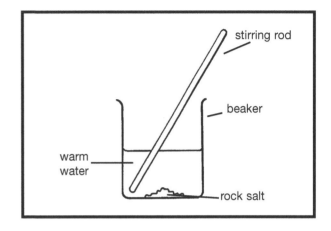

Stage 2: Filtering out the sand

○ We waited for the mixture to cool.

○ We put a filter paper inside a filter funnel.

○ We put the filter funnel over a beaker.

○ We poured the mixture into the filter funnel.

○ The salt solution went through but the sand stayed in the filter paper.

Stage 3: Evaporating the water

○ We poured the salt solution into an evaporating dish.

○ We put the dish on top of a tripod and gauze.

○ We heated the solution gently using a Bunsen burner.

○ The water evaporated and we were left with some pure salt.

Add-on

What safety equipment would you have expected Yvonne and Sahil to use during their experiment?

Electric light bulbs

Jane was investigating electrical circuits. She wanted to find out how bright the light bulb would be.

Her first circuit looked like this:

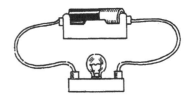

The bulb lit up, showing Jane that the circuit worked. Jane then decided to use more leads and bulbs to make two extra circuits.

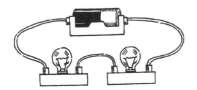 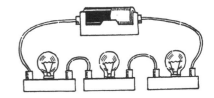

Her second circuit had two bulbs.   **The third circuit had three bulbs.**

1. What is the name given to a circuit with electrical components that are arranged one after another like these three circuits?

_____

2. What do you think will happen to the brightness of the bulbs as you add more and more bulbs? You are making a **prediction**.

_____

3. What do the following words mean?

a. Current

_____

b. Resistance

_____

4. When you are doing an investigation it is often better to try and use a piece of equipment to take measurements. What piece of equipment can you use to measure the current in each of Jane's circuits?

_____

Add-on

Looking at your prediction in question 2, can you explain why that is what you predicted? Use your answers to question 3 to explain your prediction.

Burning foods

Tom was comparing two foods: marshmallow and crisps. He wanted to see which one gave off the most heat when they were burnt.

I think the marshmallow will give off the most heat because it contains a lot of sugar.

He performed his experiment like this:

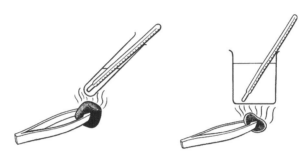

These were the results that he recorded:

Food	Starting temperature (°C)	Finishing temperature (°C)
Marshmallow	30	40
Crisp	20	40

1. Tom's teacher told him that his investigation was not fair. Make a list of the ways in which you think Tom's investigation was not fair.

   _____

   _____

   _____

   _____

2. Do you think Tom's prediction was correct?

   _____

3. If Tom's prediction was wrong then there must have been something wrong with his scientific reason or the way he had performed his investigation. Apart from doing his investigation fairly, how else do you think Tom could improve the reliability of his investigation?

   _____

   _____

   _____

Rubber bands

Priya did an experiment to see how a rubber band extends when weights are added. Her results are shown below.

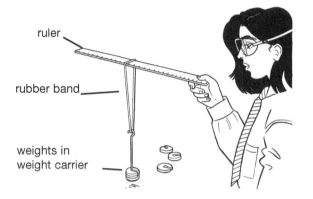

Number of weights	Extension of rubber band (mm)
0	0
1	5
2	29
3	20
4	32
5	54
6	61

1. Plot a graph of her results.

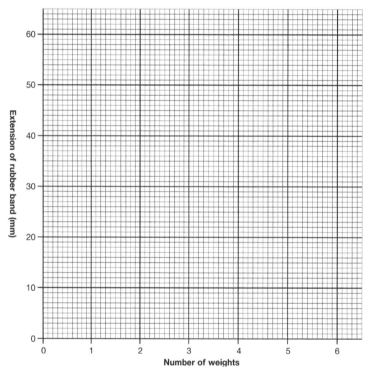

2. Decide whether the pattern is a straight line or a curve. Add a line or curve of best fit.

3. Are there any results which look odd? These are called anomalous results. If so, put a ring around them on your graph.

Add-on
What would have caused any anomolous results in the graph you have plotted?
Can you think of 2 reasons?

The seasons

The table below gives you some information about things that change during the seasons of the year.

1. Fill in the gaps in the table.

SEASON	Amount of daylight	Position of the sun in the sky at midday	Temperature
SPRING	Daylight hours increase	Fairly high	
SUMMER	Longest days Shortest nights	High	
AUTUMN		Fairly high	Days get cooler
WINTER			Coldest time of the year

2. Can you think of any other things that change with the seasons?

_____

_____

_____

_____

3. We get different seasons during the year because the earth is tilted. In the summer we are tilted more towards the sun.

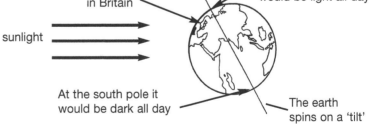

It is summer in Britain

At the north pole it would be light all day

sunlight

At the south pole it would be dark all day

The earth spins on a 'tilt'

On the picture of the earth mark a place where it would be winter.

Add-on
How could you investigate how the tilt of the earth affects temperature?
Use science books or CDs to help you come up with an idea.

Trying to slim

Clare thinks low calorie foods will help you lose weight. James thinks they are a waste of money. Can you help them investigate whether low calorie foods are any good at making you lose weight?

1. Design an investigation using Clare and James as the subjects. Use the following points to help you with your plan:

❑ Who will eat low calorie foods?
❑ What foods will they eat?
❑ How long will you need to do the investigation for?
❑ How will you measure your results?
❑ How often will you measure your results?
❑ How will you display your results?

_____

_____

_____

_____

_____

_____

_____

_____

_____

_____

2. When you do an investigation like this it is very difficult to get reliable results. When you look at your results you need to decide how reliable they are. This means deciding whether you would always get these results if you did the investigation several times.
Try to answer the following questions:

❑ Was it fair to compare low calorie foods with normal foods using Clare and James?
❑ What else might affect their weight apart from the type of foods they eat?
❑ Can you get reliable data from just two people?
❑ How many people would you have to test?

_____

_____

_____

_____

_____

_____

_____

_____

_____

_____

Circulation

Scientists and doctors have known for a long time that the heart pumps a liquid called blood around the body in tubes called blood vessels. Four hundred years ago, however, they thought the blood was pumped away from the heart along a set of blood vessels and then the blood returned to the heart along the same blood vessels.

In 1628 William Harvey described an experiment he did on the flow of blood in a human arm.

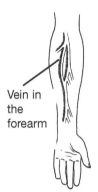

Vein in the forearm

Hold the arm downwards for a few seconds. The veins will stand out.

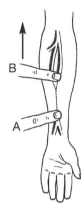

Place two fingers, A and B, on a vein near the wrist. Sweep finger B up the vein towards the elbow. This pushes blood up the vein. Lift finger B off the skin. Blood does not flow back into the vein because it never flows away from the heart.

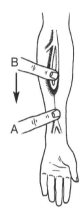

Move finger B back along the vein towards finger A. A bulge appears. This is a valve. A valve stops blood flowing away from the heart. Lift up finger A and blood will flow into the empty vein.

1. What does Harvey's experiment show about the direction of blood flow?

_____

_____

_____

_____

2. Do the results of Harvey's experiment agree with the accepted view of blood flow at that time?

_____

_____

_____

_____

3. You have been asked by your teacher to find evidence for the direction of blood flow. Where would you look: by doing your own experiments or by looking at information from books, CD-ROMs, etc?

_____

_____

_____

Add-on

Explain **why** you have chosen this source of information.

Yeast

Yeast is a type of micro-organism that is used in making bread and brewing beer. Yeast can use sugar as a source of food. As yeast uses sugar, it releases the gas carbon dioxide.

A class investigated how changing the amount of sugar affects how far up a measuring cylinder bread dough will rise.

Six different groups worked on the investigation. Shown below is a picture of the apparatus they used and a table of their results.

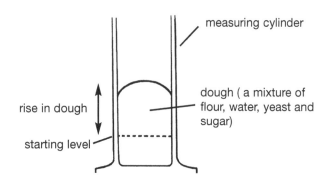

Group	Amount of sugar (g)	Rise of dough (cm)
A	5	4
B	10	6
C	15	9
D	20	10
E	25	2
F	30	10

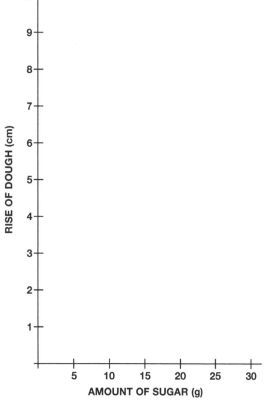

1. Use the chart to plot the results.

2. What do you think made the dough rise up the measuring cylinder?

   _____

   _____

3. To make the investigation fair, each group used the same amount of flour and the same amount of water to mix their dough. Write down three more things that the groups would need to keep the same to help make their experiment a fair test.

   a. _____

   b. _____

   c. _____

4. An anomalous result is one that is unusual. It does not fit in the pattern of the other results. Which group got an anomalous result?

Yellow fever

In the 1800's yellow fever was a common disease in Cuba. Many scientists and doctors tried to find out how it was spread from person to person. Carlos Juan Finlay was a doctor and Biologist. In 1881 he studied the disease and suggested that mosquitoes transmitted it. At first he was not believed. This activity looks at how scientific ideas are developed and changed over a period of time as new evidence is found.

1. What type of organism do you think could cause the disease yellow fever?

_____

2. Describe how you think mosquitoes could transmit the disease from person to person?

_____
_____
_____

3. Why do you think that Finlay was not believed at this time?

_____
_____
_____

Walter Reed was a Professor of Bacteriology and Microscopy. In 1900 he worked for the Cuban government to investigate the cause and transmission of yellow fever. He was able to show that Finlay was correct. He showed that it was mosquitoes that spread the disease.

4. Why do you think Reed was believed when Finlay had not been believed. What skills, knowledge or equipment do you think Reed had that Finlay didn't?

_____
_____
_____

5. If you were Walter Reed, what experiments or investigations would you do to prove that it was the mosquito that transmits the disease yellow fever.

_____
_____
_____

6. If you were to visit Cuba during this time what would you do to protect yourself from getting yellow fever?

_____
_____

Dandelions

A group of students had been asked to work out the number of dandelions growing on part of the school field. The piece of field measured 10 metres by 10 metres, so it had an area of 100 square metres. The group had a 1m square wooden quadrat to help them with the counting.

You can count the number of plants inside the quadrat

A quadrat is a wire or wooden frame. You can place it on the ground anywhere to mark out a 1 metre square

We only need to look at one quadrat. If we count the dandelions in one quadrat and multipy that by 100 then we will know how many dandelions there are in the field.

1. What do you think is wrong with this suggestion?

_____

_____

_____

_____

We need to look at 10 quadrats, along the edge of the field under the trees. If we count up those dandelions and times by 10 we will know exactly how many dandelions there are.

2. What do you think is wrong with this suggestion?

_____

_____

_____

_____

We should look at 10 quadrats in different parts of the field. The quadrats should be near the middle as well as near the edges. If we count up all those dandelions and times by 10 we will have a good estimate of how many dandelions there are.

3. Why do you think this is the best method for counting the dandelions?

_____

_____

_____

_____

Add-on

What does the word 'estimate' mean?

Element or compound?

Your teacher gives you a green powder. She asks you if this powder is an element or a compound. You have to do one or more experiments on this powder to answer your teacher's question.

1. What experiments would you do?

_____

_____

_____

2. Draw a line to link each word with the correct phrase.

Atom •   • Made up of two or more atoms joined together

Compound •   • Made up of two or more types of atom which are chemically joined

Element •   • A substance made up of only one type of atom

Mixture •   • Made up of two or more types of atom which are not chemically joined

Molecule •   • The smallest particle that all substances can be broken down into

3. Predict what you would expect to find out if the powder was an element. (Try to use some of the words and phrases above from question 2 to help with your prediction.)

_____

_____

_____

4. Predict what you would expect to find out if the powder was a compound. (Again, try to use some of the words and phrases above from question 2 to help with your prediction.)

_____

_____

_____

Add-on

What safety precautions would you take for each experiment?

Freezing points

A group of students were investigating whether salty water freezes at just one temperature and, if it does, what this temperature is.

When discussing what results to take they said:

We'll take three results

No, we need to take more than that

Where are we going to place the thermometer?

We should be able to take all the results in five minutes

No, it will take at least the whole sixty minute lesson

1. How many results do you think they should take?

_____

_____

2. Where would you place the thermometer?

_____

_____

3. How long do you think you need to take results for?

_____

_____

4. Design a results table to record your results for the investigation.

Now try the investigation yourself.

Add-on

Repeat the investigation with distilled water instead of salty water.
What differences do you notice between the two types of water?

River deposits

John and Raj were investigating river deposits. They wanted to know whether the size of sand and gravel pieces affects how far they are carried by flowing water.

They poured a mixture of water, sand and gravel into a plastic channel. After the water had stopped flowing they made a drawing and some notes about the size of the pieces of sand and gravel they found every 50cm along the channel.

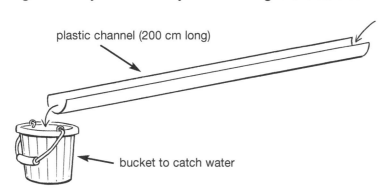

plastic channel (200 cm long)

mixture of water, sand and gravel poured here

bucket to catch water

Their results are shown in the table below.

Distance along channel (cm)	Drawing and description of deposits
0	Large pebbles
50	
100	Coarse sand
150	Fine sand
200	Very fine sand and silt

1. Some of John and Raj's results are missing. See if you can fill in the gaps.

2. Finish the sentence below to describe the pattern shown in the results.

   The _____ pieces of sand or gravel are carried _____ by the water.

3. Think of **two** other questions you could investigate about how water carries sand and gravel along. Write the questions in the spaces below.

   a. _____

   b. _____

Comparing limestone

Rob and Sara have been given pieces of two different types of limestone. They know that limestone is a type of rock that contains a lot of chemicals called carbonates. Carbonates react with acids. They have been asked to find out which type of limestone has the most carbonates in it.

Rob and Sara decide to drop acid onto the two types of limestone. After the reaction has finished they will then see how much of the limestone is left.

This is the plan for their investigation.
- Crush each piece of limestone into a powder.
- Weigh 5g of each powder.
- Put the 5g of powder in a beaker.
- Add acid a few drops at a time until the mixture stops fizzing.

Rob and Sara thought of two things that they would need to check before they did their investigation.

1. Write a few sentences to say how they could do these checks.

   a. Can we crush the limestone in a polythene bag using a hammer?

   _____

   _____

   _____

   b. Will hydrochloric acid react with the limestone?

   _____

   _____

   _____

2. Why did Rob and Sara want to crush the limestone into a powder?

   _____

   _____

   _____

3. What safety precautions should Rob and Sara take while they are doing their investigation?

   _____

   _____

   _____

4. How would Rob and Sara know which type of limestone had the most carbonates in it?

   _____

   _____

Pans

A manufacturer has designed some new 'thermal' pans. They claim that these pans heat up food more quickly than ordinary steel or aluminium pans. Their 'thermal' pans can do this because the bottom of the pan is made of copper.

Ravi decides to do an experiment to test this claim.

He uses three rods made of aluminium, steel and copper. He clamps each of the rods into a separate retort stand. He fastens four rivets onto each rod using vaseline.

Ravi then heats each of the three rods at one end. The time it takes for each rivet to fall off is shown in the table below.

Material	Time for rivet to fall off (secs)			
	1	2	3	4
aluminium	21	30	43	61
steel	38	70	95	118
copper	10	22	32	39

1. Plot a line graph of the three results on the graph paper below.

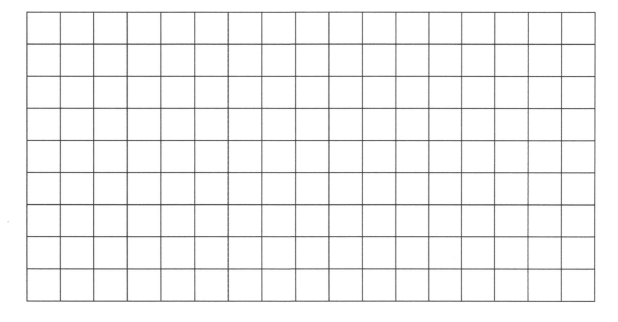

Pans (continued)

2. Was Ravi's experiment fair? If you were going to do the experiment, what would you do to make it fair?

_____

_____

_____

_____

_____

3. How would you make your results reliable? (Is one set of results enough?)

_____

_____

_____

_____

4. Do the results of Ravi's experiment support the manufacturer's claim for their 'thermal' pans?

_____

_____

_____

_____

Add-on

Do you think you can draw a conclusion about the pans from doing this experiment?
Design an experiment to test if the manufacturer's claim was true.
Explain how you would make this experiment fair and how you would
get reliable results.

Electromagnets

Joe made an electromagnet. He did this by coiling some insulated wire around a bar made of soft iron. He connected the two ends of the wire to the DC terminals of a power supply. When Joe turned the power supply on he found he could pick up some paper clips. He decided to do an investigation. He predicted what would happen.

The more coils around the iron bar, the stronger the electromagnet will be. If the electromagnet is stronger it will pick up more paper clips.

Here are Joe's results:

Number of coils	Number of paper clips picked up
5	3
10	6
15	8
20	14
25	15
30	24

Joe's results are plotted as a line graph below:

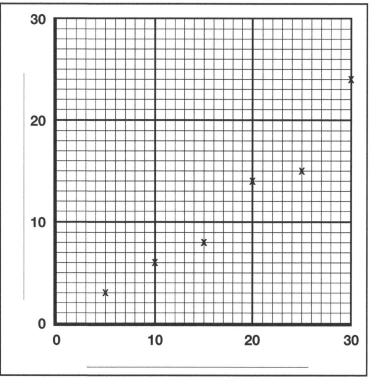

1. Add labels to each axis on the graph.

2. Joe thinks one of his results is anomalous (odd). On the graph, draw a ring around the result you think is odd.

3. Draw a line of best fit through the points Joe has plotted. Miss out the odd result.

4. Complete this conclusion:

As the number of coils increases, the number of paper clips picked up _____.

This means that _____ the number of coils makes the electromagnet

_____.

5. Was Joe's prediction correct?

Measuring reflections

Ian and Kevin investigated how light is reflected from a mirror. They shone a narrow beam of light into the mirror. They changed the angle at which they shone the light. This angle is called the angle of incidence. They also measured the angle of reflection. The diagram below shows these angles and how the boys measured the angles.

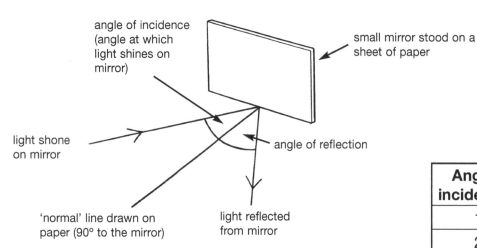

angle of incidence (angle at which light shines on mirror)

small mirror stood on a sheet of paper

light shone on mirror

angle of reflection

'normal' line drawn on paper (90° to the mirror)

light reflected from mirror

Angle of incidence (⁰)	Angle of reflection (⁰)
10	10
20	15
30	30
40	40
50	50
60	60

1. Use the results in the table to plot a graph of Ian and Kevin's results.

- ○ Label each axis.
- ○ Put a scale on each axis.
- ○ Mark each point and draw in a line of best fit.

2. Which result is an anomalous (odd) result? How might Ian and Kevin have got an odd result?

_____

_____

_____

_____

3. If Ian and Kevin had shone the beam of light at 70⁰ and then at 80⁰ what results do you think they would have got? Plot points for these extra results on your graph.

_____

Investigating hearing

We can hear lots of different sounds. Sounds can be loud or soft. Sounds can also be high or low. High sounds have a high frequency of vibration. Low sounds have a low frequency of vibration. Jo and Chris decided to investigate whether the highest frequency of sound that people can hear changes as they get older.

Jo and Chris were able to use a signal generator and loudspeaker to produce sound at different frequencies. They recorded the highest frequency each person said they could hear. They also recorded the age of each person.

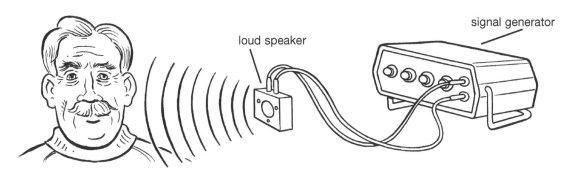

loud speaker

signal generator

Their results are shown below.

Name	Age	Frequency of highest sound they could hear
Tim	17	19,000 HZ
Dave	40	16,000 HZ
Alan	42	15,000 HZ
Eric	75	10,000 HZ

1. Which person can hear sounds with the highest frequency?

_____

2. Eric cannot hear high frequency sounds. How do you think that this could affect his everyday life?

_____

_____

3. Eric said he thought that working in a loud factory had affected his hearing. Can you suggest any other reasons why Eric's range of hearing could have changed?

_____

_____

_____

4. Jo and Chris said their results proved that when people get older they cannot hear higher frequency sounds. They also thought that you could hear fewer and fewer of these higher sounds the older you got. Their teacher said that they had not proved this. Suggest two things Jo and Chris could do to make their results more reliable.

a. _____

b. _____

Add-on

Use science books or the Internet to find out more information about how hearing changes as people get older.

Woodlice

Colin collected some woodlice. He wanted to know if the length of woodlice varies continuously or discontinuously. These are the woodlice he collected:

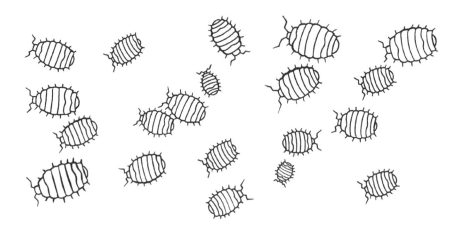

1. Measure each of the woodlice (from the tip of the antenna to the base of its back).

2. Complete this table by writing down the number of woodlice found in each category.

Number of woodlice 6 – 8mm	Number of woodlice 9 – 11mm	Number of woodlice 12 – 14mm	Number of woodlice 15 – 17mm	Number of woodlice 18 – 20mm

3. Use the results in the table to plot a bar chart of the results.

4. Does the length of woodlice vary continuously or discontinuously?

Catch it

Bert had been told that caffeine in certain drinks is a stimulant. Bert knows that a stimulant makes you more alert. Bert decided to test this by asking two of his friends to try catching a ruler.

Bert gave John a fizzy drink which did not contain caffeine. He then tested John twice with a ruler. He asked John to close his eyes and catch the ruler as soon as he felt it fall. Bert wrote down the length of the ruler that passed between John's fingers.

Bert then asked Jenny to drink some cola containing caffeine. He did the same two tests with Jenny that he had done with John. These were the results:

Bert's friend	Length of ruler passed through the fingers (cm) – first test	Length of ruler passed through the fingers (cm) – second test
John	36	32
Jenny	24	27

1. Was this a fair test?

   _____

2. If you were to make the test fair, what would you do differently?

   _____
   _____
   _____
   _____
   _____

3. Bert's teacher told him that he did not have enough evidence to make a conclusion. How would you improve the test so that there was enough evidence?

   _____
   _____
   _____
   _____
   _____
   _____

Counting bubbles

Pondweed gives off bubbles of oxygen when it photosynthesizes. Kerry and Lesley decided to investigate whether changing the amount of light affects how fast pond weed photosynthesizes.

Kerry and Lesley used the apparatus shown in the diagram below. They counted the number of bubbles of oxygen given off by the pondweed in a minute.

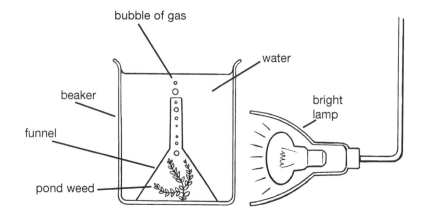

Number of lamps	Number of bubbles per minute
1	5
2	12
3	20
4	24
5	25
6	25

1. Use the results in the table to draw a line graph of Kerry and Lesley's results.

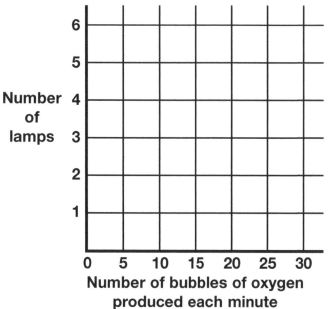

2. The points on the graph do not make a straight line. Draw a curve of best fit on your graph. This is a curve that goes through or close to as many points as possible.

3. What do Kerry and Lesley's results show about how increasing light affects photosynthesis?

_____

_____

_____

_____

4. Can you think of two other factors Kerry and Lesley could change to increase the number of bubbles produced by the pond weed?

Duckweed

Donald and Liz were investigating whether changing the amount of fertilizer in the water will affect how much duckweed grows.

They set up four identical containers. Each container had a different concentration of fertilizer in the water. They put ten duckweed plants in each container. They left all the containers for three weeks.

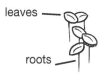

leaves

roots

Duckweed is a tiny water plant. It floats on the surface of the water

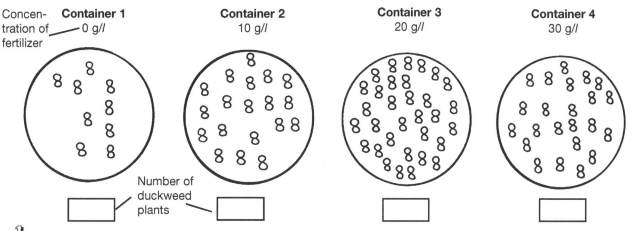

Concentration of fertilizer

Container 1
0 g/l

Container 2
10 g/l

Container 3
20 g/l

Container 4
30 g/l

Number of duckweed plants

1. The diagram above shows the containers after three weeks. Count up the number of duckweed plants in each one and write down the results.

2. What concentration of fertilizer did the duckweed grow best in?

_____

3. Write down two things that Donald and Liz did to set up a fair test.

   a. _____

   b. _____

4. Write down two more things that you would do if you were setting up this investigation to make it a fair test.

   a. _____

   b. _____

Add-on

Why do you think Donald and Liz put ten plants in each container at the start of the investigation instead of just one?

Neutralization

Harold set up the following apparatus to investigate what happens to the pH of an acid when an alkali is added.

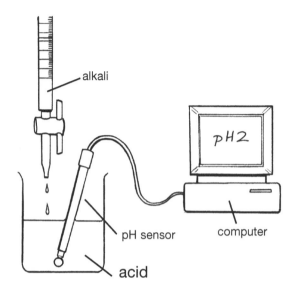

Harold wrote down the pH of the mixture after every 5cm³ of alkali added. These were his results:

Volume of alkali added (cm³)	pH of mixture
5	2
10	2
15	2.4
20	4
25	10.6
30	12.8
35	13.5
40	14
45	14
50	14

1. Plot a line graph of these results on the

graph paper.

2. What pH is a neutral solution?

_____

3. What volume of alkali did Harold need to add to the acid to neutralize it?

Add-on

Write a description for the word 'neutralize'.

Bubbles from metals

Some metals react violently when put in water. For example, sodium heats up, melts and fizzes violently on the surface of the water. Other metals don't react at all: for example, gold. All metals can be placed in a type of league table with the most reactive metals, like sodium at the top and the least reactive metals, like gold at the bottom. This league table is called the reactivity series of metals.

Howard is investigating different metals. He puts a piece of each metal into a test tube of water. After a minute he draws what each test tube looks like. These are his drawings:

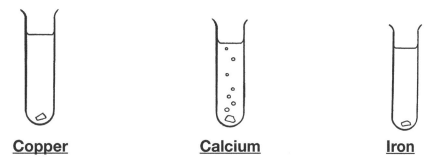

Copper   **Calcium**   **Iron**

1. Draw three more diagrams to show what you think these three metals would look like if they were placed in test tubes of dilute acid. Look in science text books to see if your diagrams are correct.

2. Howard is then asked by his teacher to predict what he would see if he put zinc and magnesium in water. Draw two diagrams to show what you think Howard predicts he will see. You will have to find out where zinc and magnesium are in the reactivity series of metals. You will be able to find this in your science book.

Add-on
Which one of these metals do you think would be best for water pipes? Explain why you have chosen this metal.

Acidic or alkaline soil

Soil can be acidic, alkaline or neutral. You can find out whether a soil is acidic, alkaline or neutral by using a soil testing kit. The kit consists of an indicator liquid which you add to the soil. The indicator changes colour to give a reading on the pH scale.

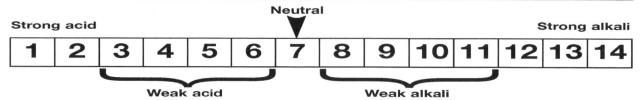

The table below shows the results of some tests on different types of soil. Use the pH scale to help you answer the questions.

Soil type	pH
Peaty soil	4·0
Sandy soil	5·0
Garden soil	6·5
'Limestone' soil	8·0

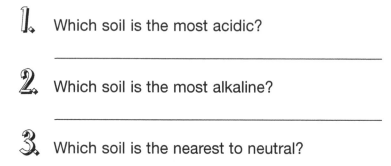

1. Which soil is the most acidic?

_____

2. Which soil is the most alkaline?

_____

3. Which soil is the nearest to neutral?

_____

4. It is important to know the pH because some types of plant will only grow well in acidic soil: for example, rhododendrons. Other types of plant may grow best in neutral or alkaline soil. Your teacher asks you to investigate whether cress seeds grow best in neutral conditions. Describe your investigation.

❑ What equipment will you need?

_____

❑ What will you change?

_____

❑ What will you keep the same?

_____

❑ How will you ensure you get reliable results?

_____

Add-on

Sometimes farmers and gardeners want to change the pH of their soil so that they can grow particular plants. What could they add to the soil to make it more alkaline? What could they add to the soil to make it more acidic?

Burning magnesium

A class of year 9 students was investigating burning magnesium. When magnesium burns it joins with oxygen from the air to make magnesium oxide. The students used a Bunsen burner to heat the crucible until the magnesium had burnt.

Here are their results:

Mass of magnesium (g)	Mass of magnesium oxide (g)
1.0	1.7
2.0	3.3
3.0	5.0
4.0	6.7
5.0	7.9
6.0	10.0

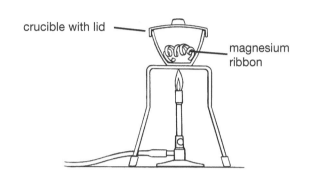

crucible with lid

magnesium ribbon

1. Use the results in the table to plot a graph for their investigation.

2. Which result does not fit the pattern shown by the rest of their investigation?

_____

3. Can you think of a reason for this anomalous result?

_____

_____

4. If you burnt 10g of magnesium how much magnesium oxide would you expect to get?

_____

Add-on
The students doing this experiment were asked to make sure that the lid was on the crucible when they burnt the magnesium.
Can you think of two reasons why they were asked to do this?

Ideas about burning

Read through the information below. Use the information and what you know about how things burn to answer the questions.

About 300 years ago scientists thought that when a material was burnt it gave off a mysterious substance called phlogiston. They knew that a candle got smaller as it burnt down. They said that this was because the phlogiston was escaping. Nobody had ever seen or been able to separate and obtain any phlogiston. Scientists thought phlogiston was invisible.

In 1772 a scientist called Joseph Priestley found a way of making pure oxygen. He did not know that the gas he had produced was oxygen but he did do some experiments using it. He found that a candle burnt more brightly if it was put in the oxygen. He also found that a mouse could live in the gas. He said, 'I have discovered a gas which is five or six times as good as common air.'

A few years later another scientist called Antoine Lavoisier was able to work out more about what happens when things burn. He weighed materials before and after they had burnt, making sure he weighed all the oxides that were produced. He found that materials were heavier after burning and said that this was because during burning materials join with oxygen from the air.

1. Early scientists looked at candles being burnt. What do you think they observed that made them think phlogiston was being given off?

_____

_____

_____

_____

_____

_____

2. What did Joseph Priestley do which showed that the oxygen he had made was involved in burning?

_____

_____

_____

_____

_____

_____

3. a. What do you think is meant by the term 'oxide'?

_____

_____

_____

_____

_____

b. Explain why you think Antoine Lavoisier found that substances had gained weight during burning.

_____

_____

_____

_____

_____

_____

4. These early scientists may have found burning difficult to understand because some of the materials produced are given off as invisible gases. Write down the names of 3 oxides that are produced as invisible gases.

_____

_____

_____

Current

Nicola was investigating the strength of the current in electrical circuits. She built four circuits.

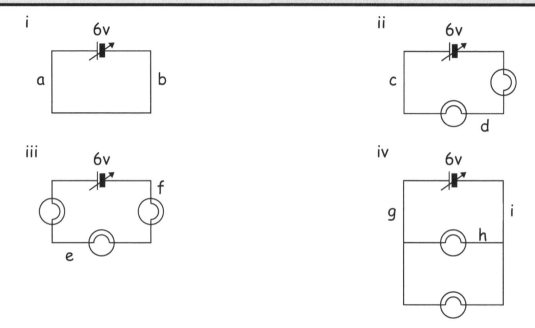

Nicola used an ammeter to measure the current at position a in the first circuit. She found out that the current was 0.05A.

Nicola's teacher then asked her to predict what she thought the current would be at points b-i in the four circuits. Nicola also had to give a reason for her prediction.

Fill in this table by writing down what you predict will happen in each case.

Circuit	Position in the circuit	Current (A)	Why?
i	a	0.05A	
i	b		
ii	c		
ii	d		
iii	e		
iii	f		
iv	g		
iv	h		
iv	i		

Gravity

Oliver's teacher, Mrs James, did an experiment to help him understand about gravity. Mrs James rolled a steel ball bearing down a slope so it followed a pencil line on some paper (see diagram 1). She then put a magnet near the line and let the ball bearing roll past. The ball bearing was attracted to the magnet and it rolled past in a curve (see diagram 2).

Diagram 1

Diagram 2

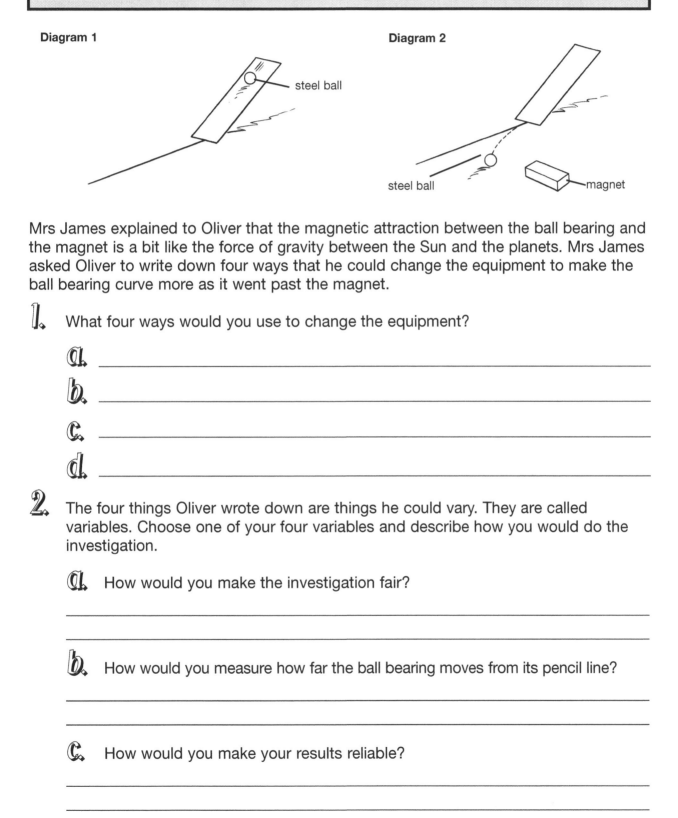

steel ball

steel ball

magnet

Mrs James explained to Oliver that the magnetic attraction between the ball bearing and the magnet is a bit like the force of gravity between the Sun and the planets. Mrs James asked Oliver to write down four ways that he could change the equipment to make the ball bearing curve more as it went past the magnet.

1. What four ways would you use to change the equipment?

   a. _____

   b. _____

   c. _____

   d. _____

2. The four things Oliver wrote down are things he could vary. They are called variables. Choose one of your four variables and describe how you would do the investigation.

   a. How would you make the investigation fair?

   _____

   _____

   b. How would you measure how far the ball bearing moves from its pencil line?

   _____

   _____

   c. How would you make your results reliable?

   _____

   _____

Parachutes

Max and Tom were investigating parachutes. They made a small parachute from some thin polythene sheet and string. They used modelling clay as a weight on the parachute. They decided to investigate whether changing the amount of weight on the parachute will change how long it takes the parachute to fall.

1. Write down two other questions Max and Tom could investigate about parachutes.

   a. _____

   _____

   b. _____

   _____

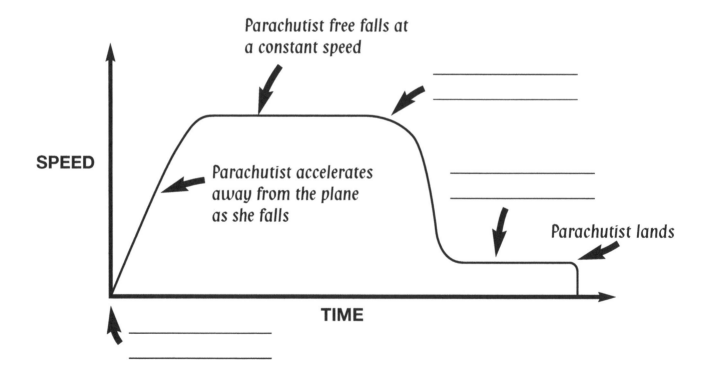

polythene sheet

string

piece of modelling clay

2. Max and Tom's teacher gave them a graph to show how the speed of a real parachutist changes during a jump. Fill in the three missing labels on the graph.

Parachutist free falls at a constant speed

_____

SPEED

Parachutist accelerates away from the plane as she falls

_____

_____

Parachutist lands

TIME

_____

_____

Add-on
Can you explain why a person making a parachute jump falls more slowly after the parachute has opened?

Turning forces

Susan and Graham had been doing some work on the 'turning effect' of forces. They had found out that for a seesaw to balance the turning effect depended on:

❍   the number of weights (force)

Susan and Graham found out that the turning force on either side of the seesaw can be worked out using this formula:

Turning force = force x distance

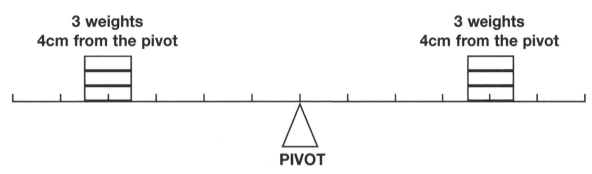

**3 weights
4cm from the pivot**

**3 weights
4cm from the pivot**

PIVOT

The see-saw is balanced

1. For the diagrams below predict where you would need to put the weights on the right-hand side of the seesaw to make it balance. Draw the weights in the correct place on the diagrams.

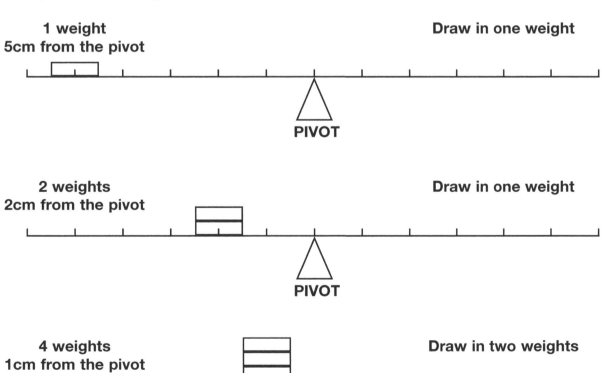

**1 weight
5cm from the pivot**   **Draw in one weight**

PIVOT

**2 weights
2cm from the pivot**   **Draw in one weight**

PIVOT

**4 weights
1cm from the pivot**   **Draw in two weights**

PIVOT

How to Dazzle at Scientific Enquiry

Turning forces (continued)

2. In the space below design a results table for the four seesaws. Your table should include columns for the numbers of weights on each side, the distance these weights are from the pivot and the two turning forces.

Also from Brilliant Publications

How to Dazzle at Being a Scientist

JEAN STANBURY

Practical activities to teach secondary pupils essential scientific skills. Over 40 photocopiable, self-contained worksheets using simple, easy-to-follow language and clear diagrams. Ideal for use with slower learners but also useful for pupils who are more able. 'Add-on' activities extend the sheets. The work relates directly to the requirements for safe procedure; obtaining evidence; analysing evidence and drawing conclusions; evaluating the evidence and recognizing anomalies.

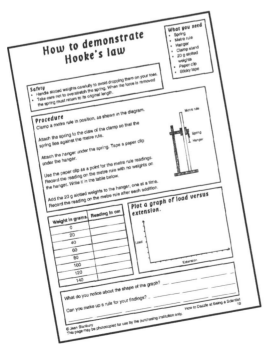

Improving Numeracy through Spreadsheets

BOB SYKES

These photocopiable sheets will help to improve pupils' numeracy skills, at the same time as teaching them some of the basic skills of using spreadsheets. The sheets can be used to enhance or introduce topic-based work in mathematics, as a springboard to open-ended ICT investigation work or simply as a confidence-boosting exercise for pupils keen to learn about the workings of their computer.

Teacher's pages with answers and advice

Other titles in the 'How to Dazzle at...' series

Science Title
How to Dazzle at Being a Scientist

Geography Title
How to Dazzle at Beginning Mapskills

ICT Title
How to Dazzle at Information Technology

Maths Titles
How to Dazzle at Algebra
How to Dazzle at Oral and Mental Starters
How to Dazzle at Written Calculations
How to Dazzle at Maths Crosswords – Book 1
How to Dazzle at Maths Crosswords – Book 2

English Titles
How to Dazzle at Grammar
How to Dazzle at Reading
How to Dazzle at Reading for Meaning
How to Dazzle at Spelling
How to Dazzle at Writing

Shakespeare Titles
How to Dazzle at Twelfth Night
How to Dazzle at Macbeth
How to Dazzle at Romeo & Juliet

Brilliant Publications sales information
Tel: 01202 712910
Fax: 0845 1309300
e-mail: brilliant@bebc.co.uk
website: www.brilliantpublications.co.uk

Lightning Source UK Ltd.
Milton Keynes UK
UKOW07f1106041115

262056UK00002B/19/P

9 781903 853153